POSTCARDS FROM PLUTO

A TOUR OF THE SOLAR SYSTEM

written and illustrated by

LOREEN LEEDY

HOLIDAY HOUSE   NEW YORK

This book is dedicated to those men and women who began the quest to explore our universe, and to those children who will someday continue the journey.

The author wishes to thank Dr. Richard C. Jones for his cosmic advice.

The author also thanks Bruce T. Draine, Professor of Astrophysical Sciences, Princeton University Observatory, for reading this book prior to its publication.

Copyright © 1993, 2006 by Loreen Leedy
All Rights Reserved
Printed and bound in October 2012 at Worzalla, Stevens Point, WI. USA.
www.holidayhouse.com
Library of Congress Cataloging-in-Publication Data
Leedy, Loreen.
Postcards from Pluto : a tour of the solar system / Loreen Leedy.
Third Edition   p. cm.
Summary: Dr. Quasar gives a group of children a tour of the solar system, describing each of the planets from Mercury to Pluto.
ISBN 0-8234-2064-7 (hardcover)
ISBN 0-8234-2065-5 (paperback)
1. Solar system—Juvenile literature. 2. Planets—Juvenile Literature. [1.
Solar system. 2. Planets.] 1. Title.
QB501.3.L44 1993 92-32658 CIP AC
523.2—dc20
ISBN-13 978-0-8234-2064-3 (hardcover)
ISBN-13 978-0-8234-2065-0 (paperback)

9 10 11 12 13 14 15

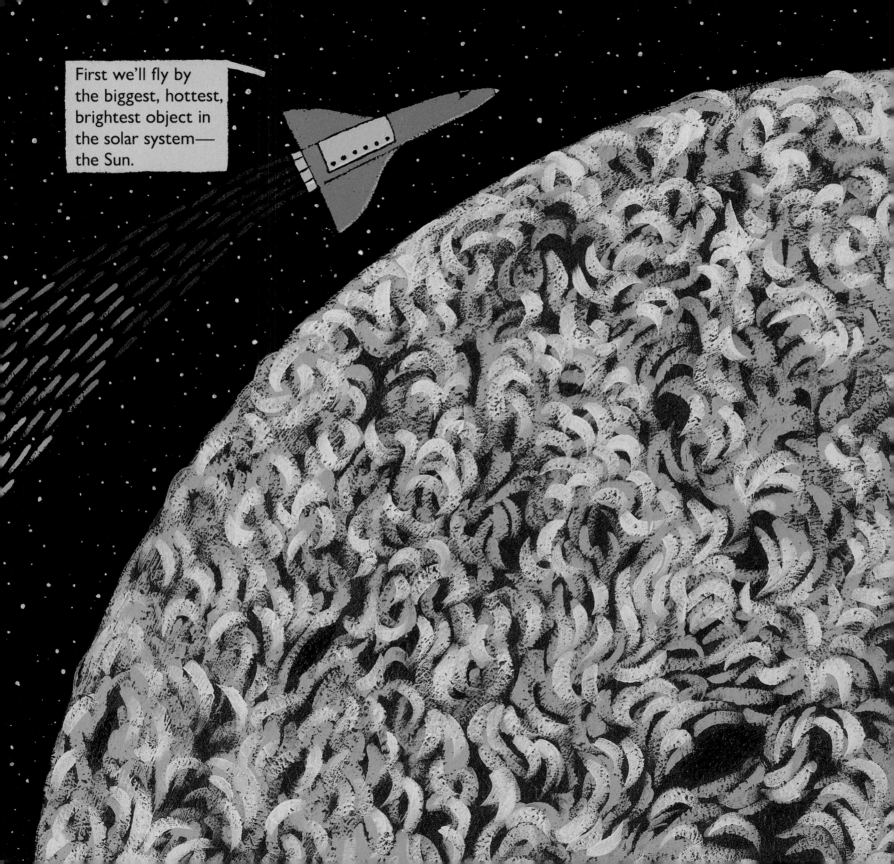

THE SUN

Dear Mom & Dad,
   Did U know that ℝ
Sun is really a ☆?
It is only a medium-
sized ☆, but over 1
million Earths could
fit in it. We can't
2 close because of the
intense heat inside.
(millions of degrees!)
   Stay cool— Your ☀
                Ray

Mr. + Mrs. Sol Corona
93 Shady Lane
Sun Valley, Idaho
U.S.A.   83353

P.S. The Sun has darker, cooler blotches called SUNSPOTS.

Dear Uncle Freddy,
GUESS THE PLANET—
1) It's closest to the Sun.
2) It has the shortest year (88 Earth days).
3) It has no water, no air, and no moons.

If you said Mercury, you're right! Also, it is burning hot on the sunny side, and freezing cold on the dark side. Good-bye for now!
Your nephew,
Eric

Freddy Fickle
100 Quicksilver Dr.
Frozenfire, Alaska
99552

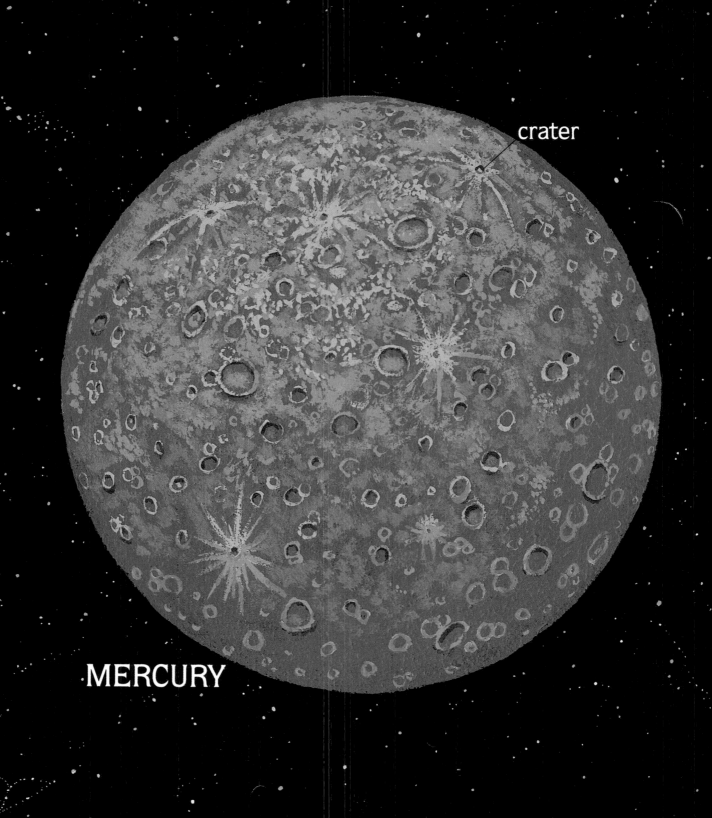

crater

MERCURY

Dear Debbie,
    We saw Venus today, and it's a little smaller than Earth, but much more dangerous. It looks like a pretty star from far away, but Venus is covered with thick, poisonous, acid clouds. There is enough heat and pressure to crack spaceships.
    Wish you were here!
        Your friend,
        Simon

Debbie DeMilo
201 Flytrap St.
Cupid City, NY
12420

VENUS

EARTH

MOON

Dear Mom,
 Guess what? We saw the
actual footprints of the first
astronaut to walk on Earth's
moon—Neil Armstrong. We left
our footprints, too. They'll
last for ages because there's
no wind or rain to destroy them.
I guess a meteor might crash
down on them. That's how the
moon's craters were made. I
hope a meteor doesn't land on us!
        Love,
            Tanisha
P.S. On Earth I weigh 72 pounds—
     here I weigh only 12!

Luna Cee
100 Crescent Ave.
Crater Lake, OR
U.S.A. 97604

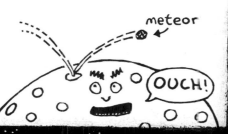

meteor

OUCH!

Earth

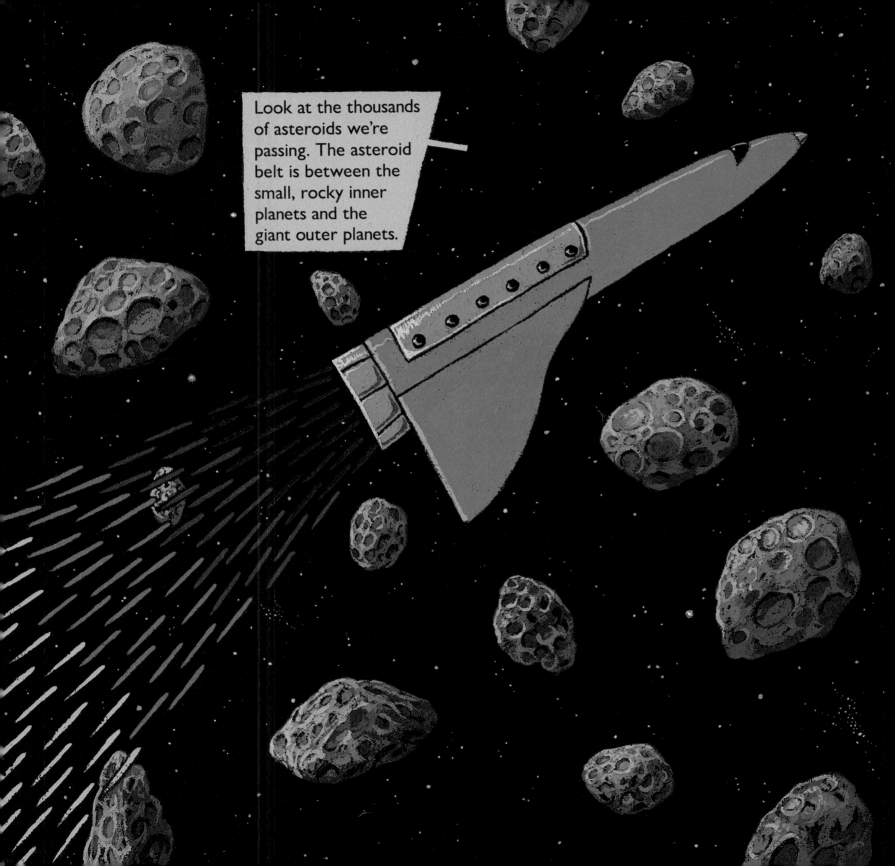

Dear Mom and Dad,
   Dr. Quasar says that
asteroids are big chunks
of rock. Most of them
stay in the asteroid belt,
but one <u>could</u> drift out
of orbit and crash into
a planet (even Earth!)
         Love,
            Simon

P.S. Don't bother wearing helmets—
the chance of an asteroid
hitting Earth is very small.

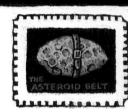

Mr. and Mrs. Goldbloom
1000 Collision Road
Bumpers, NJ
U.S.A.   08857

JUPITER is made of gases and liquids that swirl around. It has the GREAT RED SPOT which is a huge storm.

Dear Stella,
Did U know that Jupiter is the **BIGGEST** planet? It has colorful stripes, ✚ very faint rings made of dust. 👁 think the weirdest thing is that 🪐 has no solid crust of land. Maybe it is sort of like melted 🍦! ℂU later... Your bro,
Ray
P.S. 🪐 has dozens of ☾'s.

Stella Corona
93 Shady Lane
Sun Valley, Idaho
U.S.A.   83353

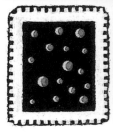

JUPITER

SATURN

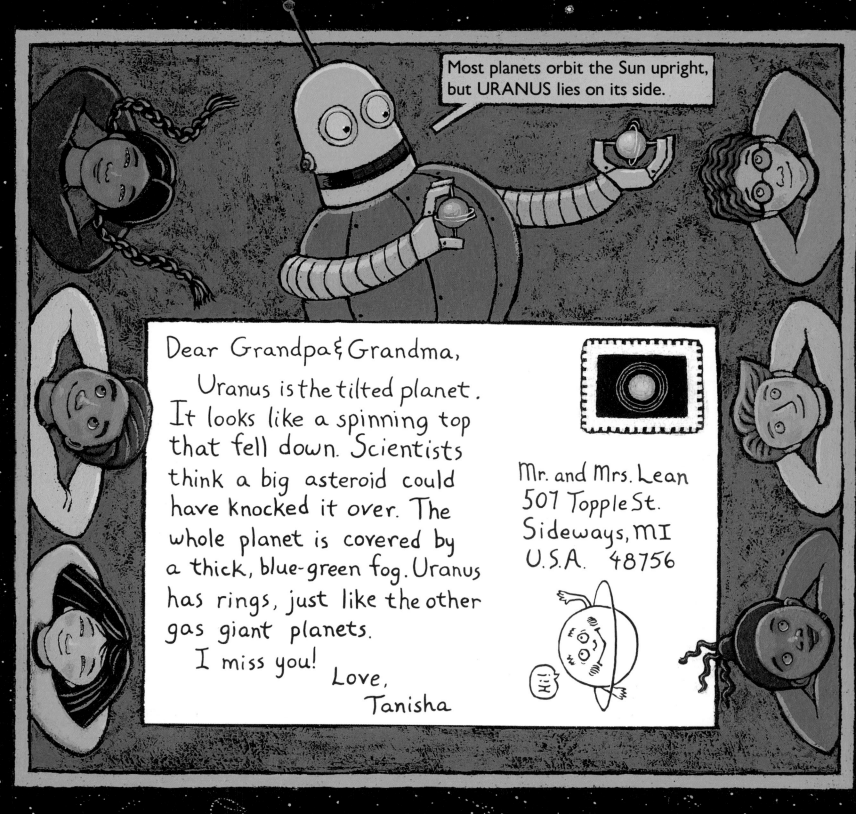

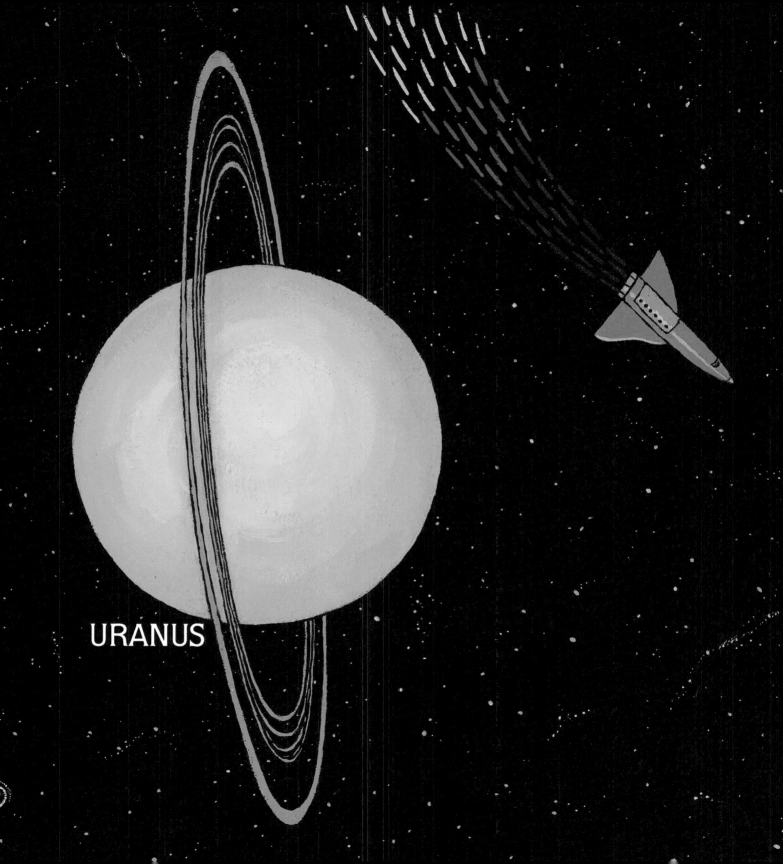

URANUS

NEPTUNE

The Sun looks so tiny from here!

...TO, ...et.

...why the outer ...are so cold.

Dear Grandfather,
Pluto is smaller than
Earth's moon. It's one of
the dwarf planets and
has moons of its own.
The biggest one is named
Charon. Can you believe
that we're 6 billion
kilometers from home?
See you soon.
        Love,
        MINDA

Joe Thunder
248 Finale Trail
Tail End, TX
U.S.A. 77050

PLANET X?

It's cold out here!

PLUTO

Charon

It's time to head back to Earth. I hope you all enjoyed your tour of the solar system.

Dear Mom ✛ Dad,
  Here Ⓡ some of the space words 👁 learned:
ASTEROID- 🪨 space rock
COMET- ☄ chunk of ice, rock, ✛ gas
CRATER- ◠ circular hollow
GALAXY- 🌀 huge group of stars
MOON- 🌑 it orbits a planet
ORBIT- 🪐 to travel around
PLANET- 🪐 it orbits a star
ROTATE- 🪐 to spin
STAR- ☀ it gives off heat and light
👁 want to visit another galaxy next, okay? ♡, Ray

Mr. ✛ Mrs. Sol Corona
93 Shady Lane
Sun Valley, ID
U.S.A. 83353